Collecting

A Beginner's Guide to Collecting Rare and Valuable Coins for Your Collection and Grading and Looking After the Coins Properly for Fun and Profit

By Jerry Haydock

© **Copyright 2020 - All rights reserved.**

The content contained within this book may not be reproduced, duplicated or transmitted without direct written permission from the author or the publisher.

Under no circumstances will any blame or legal responsibility be held against the publisher or author for any damages, reparation, or monetary loss due to the information contained within this book. Either directly or indirectly.

Legal Notice:

This book is copyright protected. This book is only for personal use. You cannot amend, distribute, sell, use, quote or paraphrase any part, or the content within this book, without the consent of the author or publisher.

Disclaimer Notice:

Please note the information contained within this document is for educational and entertainment purposes only. All effort has been executed to present accurate, up to date and reliable, complete information. No warranties of any kind are declared or implied. Readers acknowledge that the author is not engaging in the rendering of legal, financial, medical or professional advice. The content within this book has been derived from various sources. Please consult a licensed professional before attempting any techniques outlined in this book.

By reading this document, the reader agrees that under no circumstances is the author responsible for any losses, direct or indirect, which are incurred as a result of the use of information contained within this document, including, but not limited to, —errors, omissions, or inaccuracies.

Contents

Introduction: Becoming a Numismatic 1
    Learning the Ropes of Numismatics 1
Chapter 1: Where to Locate Coins..7
    Coin Shops 7
    Coin Shows...8
    Mail Orders/Web Sites...8
    Flea Markets 9
    Auctions 10
    Other Coin Collectors 10
Chapter 2: What You Ought to Search for in a Coin 12
Chapter 3: What are Mints and Mint Marks 17
    The Significance of Mint Marks. 18
    The Procedure of Minting 19
    The style 20
Chapter 4: What Impacts the Worth of a Coin?.................................22
    What Are Aspects That Impact The Worth Of Coins?..............22
Chapter 5: How to Start 27
Chapter 6: Coin Grading 32
    Strike...33
    Conservation of the Coin's Surface Area 34
    Patina or Luster..35
    Color 35
    Eye Attraction or Appeal 36
Chapter 7: Should You Utilize a Grading Service? 38

Chapter 8: When Should You Sell?...43
    The Perfect Time for Selling 43
Chapter 9: Advantages and Disadvantages of Purchasing at Auction 48
    The Advantages and Disadvantages of Auction Sales 48
    Advantages..49
    Downsides...50
Chapter 10: Commemorative and Other Special Coins 53
Chapter 11: How and Where You Can Purchase Bullion Coins......58
    Tips for Purchasing Bullion Coins 58
Chapter 12: Finding Fake Coins 63
    How to Discover Fake Coins 63
Chapter 13: How to Stay Clear of Scams 68
    Tips on How to Stay Away From Scams 68
Chapter 14: How to Look After Your Coins 73
    How to Look After Collectible Coins 73

Thank you for buying this book and I hope that you will find it useful. If you will want to share your thoughts on this book, you can do so by leaving a review on the Amazon page, it helps me out a lot.

Introduction: Becoming a Numismatic

Learning the Ropes of Numismatics

Numismatics is the study of cash, banknotes, medallions, stock certificates and token coins. It is assumed to have actually been created in the time of Julius Caesar, who composed the initial book about it. It is a really fascinating subject since each coin or medal symbolizes various periods, cultures, and economies.

Numismatists or individuals who study the history and overall look of the above-mentioned kinds of currencies, and they are distinct from coin collectors. Unlike numismatists, coin collectors are just curious about collecting coins and the prestige which comes along with it, even though; a numismatist could additionally be a coin collector and vice versa.

For many years, coin collection has actually been incredibly prominent. The most typical designs are animals and famous people and effort to illustrate the period when the particular coin was released.

Numismatists are normally curious about the use of cash, its origin, look, variety, and production. They intend to explore the function of various sorts of currency in our history by utilizing mint. Mint describes the facility or location where the coins are being produced. They additionally grade or verify coins to identify their market value. In line with this, coin grading facilities were set up.

During this time, there are 3 significant third party institutions which verify coins and/or paper currency. These are the NGC (Numismatic Guaranty Corporation) in Sarasota, Florida, PCGS (Professional Coin Grading System) situated in Newport Beach, CA and Paper Money Grading (PMG).

PCGS is a third-party organization which was created in 1986, which grades and verifies coins mainly for industrial functions. They are an independent body supplying professional viewpoints in ranking a coin. NGC is additionally a third party organization providing services entirely to Numismatists. It was created in 1987. Meanwhile, PMG is exclusively for paper money authentication and a tinier PCGS department.

Back when coin collecting wasn't as prominent as now, there were just 3 classifications to which a coin might fall.

1. Good-- which implies that the coin has all the particulars unscathed

2. Fine-- which indicates that the coin has all the particulars unscathed and still has a little luster noticeable and

3. Uncirculated-- which indicates that the coin was never ever placed up in the market, therefore, preserving its initial look.

Nevertheless, these days coin grading has actually progressed and is ending up being more definite. They utilize a mix of numbers and letters that represent the coin quality. Right now, the coin grading system of the United States is the simplest and is advised for novices. Instance of U.S.A. grading system: MS-60 to MS-70, which suggests that the coin is blemish-free and has excellent strike and color. In other words, it's superb!

Understanding how to grade a coin effectively is not just a gift, it's an art. It demands understanding, exposure, and capabilities. For coin collectors, the capability to grade a coin is a must since the worth of a coin mainly depends on it.

Here are some components numismatists utilize in coin grading. We are going to discuss this even more in an approaching chapter.

1. Luster - it is an identifying element to see if a particular coin has actually been distributed or not. To have a greater grade, a coin needs to be technically unscathed and devoid of any kind of blemish or imperfection.

2. Surface area conservation. Abrasion on the coin's surface is a substantial factor when it comes to grading a coin. However, it does not always indicate that abrasion is able to reduce the coin grade. For instance, if an attractive coin has a serious abrasion on the rear but undetectable, it is going to not count versus the coin. However, the problem might not be identical if the abrasion lies on the front or focal point.

3. Strike. It describes the coin creating procedure in which the coin is stamped onto a planchet. In general grading, the strike is not really heavy.

4. Coloration. For certain coin collectors, conservation of the initial coin color has a substantial effect on its worth, particularly if it is a silver or copper coin.

5. Eye appeal. Some coins might not be ideal; however, others might find it appealing. Nevertheless, it still needs a professional opinion to conclude that a particular coin is outstanding in all elements discussed.

If you know nothing about grading coins, you should not start with numismatics and coin collecting without using aid from the professionals. Coins have actually been playing an essential function, not just in the lives of individuals who like studying and collecting them yet additionally in society, for they represent a period in the history of people. Whether you are selling, purchasing, or collecting, it does not hurt to obtain fundamental understanding or information.

Chapter 1: Where to Locate Coins

Coin collecting has actually begun just as a pastime for many people. Nevertheless, you can hear other individuals state (or you most likely have actually heard them yourselves) about the stories of individuals earning money with their old coins. That inspired more individuals to go on a coin-collecting journey. If you are among those individuals who wish to buy coins, here are numerous locations to begin your collection.

Coin Shops

A number of store owners are dealers who understand a great deal about the coins and are selling certain coins as well. These coin stores are an important location to discover and find out more about coin collecting and coins. These coin stores could be expensive as they are seeking to sell their coins for a profit. With adequate understanding and/or having somebody who understands a lot about coin collecting by you, you can get terrific prices.

Coin Shows

There are times when your neighborhood mall is going to have a display from a number of coin dealers. These are going to allow you to see their collection and enable you to get a few of them for a lower price because of competitors. You are going to most likely additionally see a number of brand-new coins that are up for grabs and great for your collection.

These coin shows are fantastic, not just for purchasers yet additionally for coin aficionados who wish to see uncommon and tough to locate coins.

Mail Orders/Web Sites

There are countless dealers around the world, and the majority of them have sites that enable you to pay them via mail order or via any internet payment system like PayPal. You ought to conduct your research on these businesses and read their terms thoroughly to make certain that you can get your cash back when you have issues with the coin you got.

For one genuine website, there are most likely numerous phony websites which are simply aiming to get your cash. You ought to ask for some feedback prior to paying anyone online and keep in mind not to give out any pin numbers or passwords.

Flea Markets

This sort of location is an unexpected location to discover uncommon coins. Nevertheless, these locations have various notions of prices, which is so because of their absence of understanding of coin pricing. You are going to discover pricey coins, however, if you are fortunate, you may discover an uncommon coin someplace in those stacks of coins, and that is going to make it worth your time.

Flea markets sellers are typically searching for a fast sale and would most likely offer you discounts when you purchase their products in bulk. Try to purchase other products and get your coin included as a reward.

Auctions

If you want to invest in truly, truly uncommon coins, the ideal location to go would be in an auction. Auctions are the only locations where you may discover individuals selling their rarest and most pricey coins.

Lots of these auctions are occurring on the web, and the majority of the sellers are searching for the best bidders. Nevertheless, you need to be cautioned that a few of these sellers are scams and are not going to make the price you pay rewarding. You ought to attempt to find out more about these coins and their value prior to attempting to purchase one from an online auction.

Other Coin Collectors

Coin collectors generally have replicate coins that they want to sell for a lower price than its market price. The only issue is that it is difficult to discover another coin collector like you. The very best locations to look are forums, online groups, and neighborhood groups. Other coin collectors are the ideal individuals to go to when you wish to begin your own collection. They can provide you with suggestions, discount rates, and some may even be enticed to provide you with a few of their coins to kick-start your collection.

Coin collecting is similar to every other investment. They depreciate in worth, and other coins may experience an uphill climb. The ideal method to profit with coin collecting is to be up-to-date with the news and the routine coin prices. These are going to not just assist you in not being deceived by numerous merchants yet additionally with finding out how to price a coin even without a catalog.

Chapter 2: What You Ought to Search for in a Coin

Coin collecting is an enjoyable pastime to begin. The excitement of searching for old coins is enough for lots of people to keep on doing it. Other individuals, however, consider coin collecting as a financial investment, something they are able to profit with.

A lot of coin collectors would search for just a particular type of coin. These are going to make their collection more worthwhile and intriguing for purchasers. Others are collecting coins for sentimentality and are paying more attention to the coin's originality.

Series collectors are those individuals wanting to get one of every date for each time a coin was minted. They are aiming to get a coin which marks each design change and each year. Type collectors are those individuals aiming to acquire one of each coin with changes.

Ancient coin collectors are those individuals searching for coins between 650 BC and 450 AD. This is when coins were created, and there were goldm silver and bronze variations of them. It additionally marks the period when Roman emperors were the rulers, and the majority of them include well-known Roman towns, Roman emperors and gods.

Token collectors are those trying to find various types of tokens that were utilized in exchange for real cash where there is an absence of coins. These tokens were utilized as local currency even if the government has not permitted its utilization.

Coins are additionally graded. A coin's grading depends upon its condition, and the coin price is going to rely greatly on it. It is very crucial for a coin collector to understand how to grade a coin to ensure that he is not tricked by people wanting to make a fast buck.

Uncirculated coins are coins without any tear and wear or to utilize a well-known term, are in mint condition. A mint state (MS) grading is based upon contact marks, luster, hairlines, and general appeal. A coin could have a grade varying from MS-60 (dull luster) to a perfect MS-70. Even though MS-70 is looked at as unobtainable, a grade of MS-65 and greater are going to make a coin's price skyrocket.

Circulated coins are more flexible; it does not consider the amount of dirt and scratches a coin has actually collected throughout the years. Circulated coins grades are going to differ. AU (about uncirculated), EF (extremely fine), VF (very fine), F (fine), VG (very good), G (good), AG (about good), F-2 (fair) and P (poor) are utilized as an indicator of just how much a coin is worth.

These grades depend on a circulated coin's luster, noticeable wear, style aspects, and presence of letters and characters. Unlike uncirculated coin's grades, however, these grades do not drastically reduce a coin's worth. This is fantastic for individuals who are looking simply to finish a collection and aren't bothered with mint condition.

The pricing of a coin is going to depend on a coin's supply and demand. Extremely low supply and extremely high demand are going to make a coin's price shoot higher. Nevertheless, the high supply of coins is going to lower a coin's worth.

Demand is generally developed by coin dealerships where they take into account individuals wishing to purchase coins and the variety of individuals selling them. When a coin ends up being challenging to discover, coin dealers are going to normally make its price higher in such a way that it is going to make more individuals willing to sell additional coin copies.

Grading and pricing a coin typically takes a great deal of experience to master. Even though there are numerous suggestions and standards to keep an eye out for in coin grading, just professional dealers have the last word on just how much is a coin's worth. It does not hurt, however, to understand that this grading is performed and why your coin was graded in a different way from what you have seen.

Coin collecting is not truly about financial investment; it ought to be an enjoyable and thrilling pastime. While the general objective of a coin collector is to finish a coin set, discovering what to try to find in a coin is essential to ensure that nobody can benefit from your requirement to finish a specific set.

Chapter 3: What are Mints and Mint Marks

Mint Marks are small letters describing the locality where the coin minting happened. The mintmark position could be discovered normally on the rear of coins that were minted prior to 1965 with the exception of the cents and at the front after 1967.

Coins of each US mint branch are acknowledged by mint marks. These marks go way back to times of Greece and Rome. The Mint Director through "Act of March 3, 1835", established guidelines to categorize and differentiate the coins released from each "United States Mint branch." This core management made precise patterns and standards of production along with accountable coinage.

Coins that reached the "Philadelphia mint" much before 1979 don't have mint marks. So that was the year in which the dollar was marked using the letter P and other denominations had that identical mark afterward.

All Dies for United States coins are created at the "Philadelphia Mint," and before delivering the coins to their mint branch, coins are marked initially with the appropriate and appropriate mint markings. The exact positioning and size of the mint mark could differ a little; this is affected by the depth and location of mint impression.

The Significance of Mint Marks.

Collectors can figure out the worth of a coin via mintmark, condition and date evaluation, where the coin's condition is the most considerable aspect and requirement to determine its worth.

On the other hand, specifying the Mint, which struck the coin, is enormously essential too. To determine the worth of the coin, the coin could be struck in substantial amounts at a single Mint and minute amounts in another hit.

The Procedure of Minting

1. The metal strip creation in the proper density. Zinc strips are utilized for cents, alloy strips made up of nickel (25%), and nickel (75%) for nickel and dollars, dimes, half-dollars, half-dimes are produced from a combination of 3 coatings of metals. The external layer is composed of alloys, and the middle is made of copper.

2. These metal strips are then placed into "blanking presses" that handle the cutting of "round blanks," roughly to the dimension of the "completed" coin.

3. The blanks are then run through an annealing furnace in order to soften them, via barrels toppling and finally via revolving cylinders, including chemical mixes to clean up and burnish the metal.

4. The blanks then are, after that, cleaned and put into a drying device, and then put in the "upsetting" machines which generate raised rim.

5. The last stage: "coining press." Every blank is clasp in place by a ring or collar as it is being hit or struck using a lot pressure. Cents require 40 tons of pressure, and a lot larger coins require more. The "Upper and lower dies" are marked all at once on the two coin sides.

The style

The "Director of the Mint" selects the pattern and design for US coins that are then authorized by the "Secretary of the Treasury"; congress could suggest and suggest a style. The style then can not be altered until each 25 years of gap or unless that is decided by the congress.

All symbols of US coins minted presently show former US presidents. President Lincoln at the one-cent coin embraced in 1909; Washington at the 25 cent coin which was minted initially in 1932; Jefferson at the 5 cent coin in 1938; Franklin Roosevelt on the dime, presented in 1946; Kennedy half-dollar which initially emerged in 1964.

The "Act of 1997," referred to as the "50 States Quarters Program," supports the quarter redesigns, where the reverse side is to show every one of the fifty states symbols.

The expression "In God We Trust" was initially utilized on a US two-cent coin in 1864. It then was located on the nickel, quarter, silver dollar, half-dollar and on $10, $20, and $5 in 1866; in "1909 on the cent", in "1916 on the dime". Nowadays, all US coins hold the slogan.

Chapter 4: What Impacts the Worth of a Coin?

What Are Aspects That Impact The Worth Of Coins?

When one is simply beginning with collecting coins, the question is: What is the worth of the coin? Your coin is going to cost as much as whichever quantity somebody wants to pay for it. The quantity could differ substantially. For example, coin dealers' offer could be much smaller than that of a coin collector that desires your coin to add it to his collection.

The following are aspects which could affect the true worth of a coin.

1. Coin condition or grade. Your coin is going to be valued or worth more when it is of fine condition. When in unblemished or perfect mint condition, an "uncirculated coin" is going to be worth many times more when in comparison to a coin of a comparable state which has gone into circulation.

2. Rareness remains, in reality, the primary basis of a coin's worth. Normally, the rarer that a coin is, the higher it is priced. Nevertheless, bear in mind that rareness has extremely little impact on the coin's age.

Numerous Chinese coins aging a thousand years usually sell for around 10 dollars, given that there are a lot of them all over, whilst a "1913 Liberty Head Nickel" could sell for nearly or above a million dollars, considering that just 5 of them are known to exist.

3. Bullion value. A coin's precious metal material could identify its worth. A platinum, gold, or silver coins are not going to, in general, sell under the coin value when melted.

4. Demand. There are coins which are considerably in demand; searched for by plenty of collectors. The more that a specific coin remains in demand, the higher it is priced. Even relatively abundant coins can mandate greater worth when they are prominent with collectors.

For example, "1916 D dimes" are quite plentiful in comparison to the "1798 dimes". Yet in spite of this, "1916 D dimes" sell a lot more, because there are many people collecting 20th-century dimes instead of 1700 dimes.

Here's how you may figure out the approximate coin worth:

1. Appropriately, precisely and correctly acknowledge and categorize your coin, as you ought to understand what you intend to put worth on. You may do this effectively by analyzing your coin in a catalog or online price guide; this is going to offer you an idea of the prices and going ratesfor your specific coin.

Daily coin values are altering; so you want to utilize a "coin price guide" that is revised daily, so you can acquire fresh and present coin values. Additionally, take a look at websites which provide step by step directions on how to evaluate your coin the correct way.

2. Grade your coin based upon your comprehensive observation and assessment of its present condition.

3. Use coin catalogs in order to stumble upon a retail selling pricelist or coin retail worth estimates. "A Guide Book of United States Coins" or commonly called "The Red Book" supplies details about coin prices in retail for United States coins, and it is obtainable in libraries, coin stores, and book shops. "The Standard Catalog of World Coins" (in volumes) is a guide typically utilized by coin collectors and dealers to offer information on world coins, located in a number of public libraries.

You can additionally inspect present coin prices based upon the true dealer coin price on publications or online auctions like Coin World, eBay, or Teletrade.

Constantly bear in mind that you are not collecting coins mainly for cash; you collect for self-gratification, and cash needs to come in last. That is why the plain reality that a specific coin does not have a big financial worth does not always imply that it is no longer interesting or that it should not be a part of your collection.

Each coin is going to have a specific interest in itself, despite the state that it remains in, despite its financial worth. There is going to constantly be that particular quality that is going to draw you to that specific coin, so when it does, then it is recommended to have it in your collection. Have a good time!

Chapter 5: How to Start

There are numerous reasons why someone collects coins. There are collectors who collect due to the coin's perceived future value, some folks collect coins originating from simply one specific duration, some do it because of the type of metal and some for a coin's historic worth.

There are additionally those who delight in collecting regular typical coins, getting enjoyment from examining dates and mint marks on their daily change. Others have a coin collections originating from various nations. Some coin collectors invest thousands in uncommon silver and gold coins from the duration in the 1800s to the duration in the early 1900s.

The coin collecting hobby could provide satisfaction and fun to a person at any age. Numerous coin collectors started their collection when they were kids, collecting dimes or cents. Actually, there are people who turned coin collection into a lifetime pastime.

The pastime of coins coins includes spending cash from the beginning, so it is excellent to sign up with a coin collector group so one can get ideas and assistance from well-informed and skilled collectors.

You want someone to purchase your coins from, and it might be tough to discover a coin dealership of good reputation when you are brand-new to the pastime, so having somebody who remains in this pastime for many years could be of fantastic assistance to assist you with selecting a sincere and well-informed coin dealer.

Begin by obtaining a huge magnifying glass and take a look at coins in a bright location so you could identify errors, mintmarks, and to plainly read dates on damaged or worn coins. Choose which coins to gather and purchase a "bookshelf folder" for that series.

You need to have storage, like clear tubes created from plastic or coin tubes that have screws to keep your coins in up until such time when you are ready to place them in a coin album. Storage can additionally be great for keeping replicate coins.

There is a requirement for you to learn about various coin values. Follow what kinds of coins are offered, and what are they priced based upon dealership prices. You are additionally going to require somebody or some references which are going to reveal to you how to examine the precise worth of a specific coin based upon age, mint mark, surface area, color and condition.

"A Guide Book of United States Coins" or generally called "the Red Book," which is released annually, supplies a great summary of U.S. coins history, information on fundamental coin grading, coin descriptions from previous to present consisting of a list of mistakes to look out for, typical U.S. coins retail expense and explanation of mistakes which took place in the "minting procedure." Month-to-month publications from "Coinage" (coin collecting publication) include numerous helpful truths and information in addition to articles about your new pastime plus plenty of fantastic pictures.

The newspaper, especially in the numismatic world area, is going to be of interest to you, particularly when you end up being increasingly more involved and interested in your pastime and would wish to stay updated about the present happenings in the numismatic world.

As you grow more skilled in collecting coins, your "eye for coins" is going to get better and establish maturely; hence you are now going to be inspecting features and particulars like coin letterings more thoroughly, ensuring that the letters are not blurred or blemished, yet still distinct.

Similarly, you are going to be paying so much interest and focus to the coin's basic state, and you could wander away from specific coins that have a lot of apparent abrasion marks, therefore, you are going to be experiencing the enjoyable coin collecting side.

Invest enough time in reading, looking at pictures, learning from skilled collectors, and asking as many questions which require some clarification from not simply other collectors, yet dealers too. The pastime of collecting coins is a continuing procedure; it is going to go on for as long as you are into the pastime.

Your understanding and training are going to spare you a great deal of cash in addition to making you cash when the time arrives. However, more significantly, have a good time while learning. Get a kick out of what they name the "Hobby of Kings."

Continue learning, since the better your understanding is, the more that you are going to delight in your new-found pastime.

Chapter 6: Coin Grading

A "grade" is a shorthand developed by coin specialists (numismatists) to expose a coin's look. Basically, if a particular coin collector informs another collector that he has an uncirculated Charlotte 50 half eagle, both ought to currently have an idea of the look of the coin without even laying eyes on it, due to the claim of its grade.

Some divulge that designating a grade to rank or classify a coin is more of an art as opposed to science given that it is usually very biased or subjective; this is especially true when dealing with "Mint State" coins in which little distinctions in regards to grade mean a lot when it comes to the price.

Still, grading could be studied, learned and used with foreseeable and recognized results that ultimately depend upon judgment, not sensations.

Therefore, such as any language, sport, science, or research, it is ideal to discover and comprehend coin grading with one element at once, via experience and study.

Nowadays, a lot of numismatists utilize the "Sheldon grading scale." While there are those who experience "too many grades," experienced coin graders acknowledge and value the reality that there is a large variety in features between ranges.

Strike

This is the approach of marking or inscribing a drawing or a sign onto a blank. Depending upon the coin's style, it could either have a strong or weak strike. An instance of this would be the "Type II gold dollar," where two sides (reverse and obverse) have the greatest strike which is completely aligned. Meaning, these styles need weak strikes.

In general, the strike is truly not a crucial factor in developing the grade of a coin other than when it is included in a series in which value is linked to strike.

Conservation of the Coin's Surface Area

The variety of coin mark preservation along with where they are positioned is a substantial aspect of developing the grade. While there is no set formula on the coin mark number which sets its grade, there are a number of regulated requirements concerning the importance of the positioning or location of a scratch.

For example, a coin having a deep scratch that is concealed well on its reverse is not going to be strictly punished Nevertheless, if the identical scratch was placed on an obvious or apparent main point on the front, like the Statue of Liberty cheek, it is going to be penalized substantially more.

Patina or Luster

A coin could have a range of surface textures, affected by design, the metal which was utilized, and the "mint of origin." Textures could feature wintry, prooflike, satiny and semi-prooflike.

When analyzing the coin's surface area in regards to grade, 2 things ought to be considered; the amount or what is left of the initial skin (needs to be undamaged) and the place and quantity of marks.

Luster is essential, specifically when figuring out whether a coin is either uncirculated or circulated. A coin in Mint State is without wear and abrasion and should not have considerable luster breaks.

Color

This is an extremely subjective aspect of identifying coin grade. For example, a "gold coin" revealing dark green-gold coloring might be unappealing to one collector and appealing to another.

As gold is reasonably an inert metal, it is not vulnerable to much color variation as silver or copper. Still, full-scale colors might exist in gold coins.

Nearly all US gold coins had actually been dipped or cleaned up, and for that reason, they are not showing their initial color any longer. As collectors end up being experienced, the majority of them are drawn in and captivated by coins having their natural color. In a lot of coin series, it is almost inconceivable to find initial coin pieces.

Eye Attraction or Appeal

Color, strike, luster and surface area marks make up "eye appeal." Keep in mind that a coin having exceptional "eye appeal" could be strong in one element, like luster yet not as strong in another element, like color.

A coin which is unfavorable in one element yet sufficient in all the other elements could still be differentiated as "second-rate" in "eye appeal." Understanding how to grade a coin is quite crucial, so one could have an idea of the worth or a coin price that he is purchasing or offering. So when brand-new to collecting coins, make sure to ask for the assistance of a knowledgeable collector when purchasing or exchanging coins.

Chapter 7: Should You Utilize a Grading Service?

Collecting coins has actually been a prominent pastime for many individuals of all ages. The marketplace of coins has actually expanded extensively. Nevertheless, due to this broad market, the coin prices have actually differed profoundly.

Previously, the coin market was restricted to a tiny number of dealers and collectors. Coins were priced in easier terms. Nevertheless, while the marketplace broadened, dealers have actually been really irregular with the prices they set for the coins. This was when the requirement for a basic scale arose. That is where the coin grading services have actually appeared on the scene.

Coin grading services have the ability to supply services that are going to set basic practices which are really crucial in the market. Any collector who sees the large market of coins is going to see the value of a grading service. Numerous dealers overgrade the coins which they offer, and that is why coin collectors have to be familiar with this.

Coin grading services have basic scales for each coin spread around the marketplace. One advantage it supplies is that coins are going to be evaluated fairly and properly. Antique coins and uncommon ones are going to be scaled depending upon their quality, origin and the reason for their release.

A coin collector might have to get a coin grading service when purchasing a coin. This is going to examine the credibility of the coin and if the coin is priced fairly. Sellers, on the other hand, utilize the grading service to inspect if they can produce earnings based upon the price they have actually set on the particular coin. This is going to additionally make sure that the price dealers establish is not too high and is close to the real coin value.

Lots of collectors are victims of scams, specifically when purchasing uncommon coins. A grading service is going to guarantee that the coin is not a fake one, and this is going to protect against scams in each negotiation.

Coins might change their worths across time. The grading service is going to make sure that the coin is going to have the updated price. It is going to additionally evaluate if a coin might lose its worth depending upon some aspects such as the look of the coin.

A few of the reliable grading services are the PCI, PCGS, NGC and Anacs. These services have great records and are recognized to offer important and valuable services. These services offer constant and precise lead to grading.

They rarely or never ever have been reported to be over grading. They are additionally recignized for their proficiency in inspecting the coin authenticity precisely. Other essential elements are additionally looked at by these services, like discovering any marks and issues with the coins and changes in the mintmarks and dates. Coin grading services are additionally able to find if there was cleansing, toning and fixing work that was done on the coins which were graded.

Coin grading services could additionally assist if there are scams and prohibited activities which are being performed by dealers. They have hotline numbers where customers are able to call and report any unlawful activity. This is going to guarantee that customers are safe with the coin grading services.

Grading services could additionally ensure the credibility of the coin. With these services such as the ones used by PCGS, grading is performed with at least 3 professionals. This remains in accordance with the requirements set in their policies. If a customer believes that he was still over graded, he could bring back the coin and constantly have it regarded to make sure all information provided was fair and precise.

Coin grading services offer grade guarantees. Unlike dealerships, they do not supply this benefit. Dealers are just able to supply viewpoints on grade; however, they are not able to guarantee them.

As coin collectors, individuals have to guarantee that they get what is fair for them. The grading services exist to assist and help these collectors. Coin collectors have to be knowledgeable about the advantages of grading services and must not just depend on viewpoints originating from dealers.

In selecting a grading service, it is suggested to inspect the reliability of the service constantly. It is ideal to examine the Web to confirm information relating to a specific coin grading service. Awareness is a really special aspect of ensuring security amongst collectors.

Chapter 8: When Should You Sell?

The Perfect Time for Selling

When is the best time to offer coins? This might be a stupid question if posed to a collector. Nevertheless, this time truly happens. There are times when a collector gets up in the early morning, and all of a sudden, decides to sell his valuable coin collection.

There are additionally times when a collector has to quit his coin collections because of some private factors, and the idea of offering his valuable coins might appear to be the most challenging part.

There are lots of reasons why collectors decide to sell their coins. There are collectors who are dealers simultaneously. Offering coins is how they get the coins they like.

Some collectors travel looking for a coin they desire. Throughout travel, they might come across coins which might not be qualified for their own collection; however, they purchase them anyhow. Once they arrive home, they offer the coins they have actually purchased and utilized the cash to purchase the coins they are searching for.

There are additionally coin collectors who collect coins not just as their pastime. These collectors utilize the coins as their income source. They earn a living with the coins that they gather. They offer the coins to other collectors and set the higher price than the typical price of the coins.

This is most suitable if the collector owns small editions or uncommon coins.

Meanwhile, certain collectors sell their coins due to some other things. They might sell coins due to some individual reasons. There are collectors who opt for handing out their collection due to the fact that they no longer have any choice. This is the toughest situation for collectors.

Coin collectors frequently value their coins and would not give them away. The coins might be keepsakes to them, or they may have nostalgic value to the collector.

When a collector has actually chosen to offer his coins, he needs to initially think about if it is truly the correct moment for selling. Is the collector prepared to give away the coins? Is the coin at a greater price now? Is it going do well, and is he going to profit from selling the coins? These elements ought to constantly be thought about.

There are other alternatives when it comes to selling the coins. He might wish to sell the coins at auctions. Many individuals now choose the alternative of putting their possessions at auction sales, and this is not restricted to collections.

There is additionally a greater opportunity of having actually the coin sold at a greater price because auctions consist of bidding procedures. Purchasers might bid for a greater price, specifically if the coin being offered is of uncommon quality and has a greater worth.

A collector might additionally wish to set up a site to market the coins that he wants to offer. The Web is the most convenient way where collectors look for coins. Additionally, placing the coin on the web is going to make selling a simpler job. The collector might set up his own site and place the pictures of his coins and some short descriptions of them. He could additionally keep in mind just how much he wants to sell them.

Other alternatives might additionally be considered. The seller might wish to carry out a dealer-to-dealer negotiation. He could go straight to coin dealerships to sell the coins. The dealers can then sell the coins sold to them.

Nevertheless, it is essential to compare prices initially between dealers. It is possible that some dealers might purchase the coins for a higher price. It is just a good idea to look for dealers, and after that, select to whom to sell the coins.

It is additionally advised that collectors who choose to sell their coins get a coin grading service. This is really crucial so that the seller doesn't wind up as a loser as soon as he sells the coins. With the grading service, the seller is going to have the ability to set a price which is based upon the evaluation performed by the grading service. A grading service is going to rank the real worth of the coins.

Most significantly, the coin collectors must not clean their coins once they have actually chosen to sell them. Otherwise, the worth of the coins is going to go down.

Chapter 9: Advantages and Disadvantages of Purchasing at Auction

The Advantages and Disadvantages of Auction Sales

In a collection of coins, the hardest part is how to discover the coins for the collection. A collector's primary technique of obtaining coins is purchasing them. The most typical alternative to obtaining a coin is via purchasing in auction sales.

Uncommon coins and those which have top quality are really tough to purchase. Auction sales, whether at actual auction houses or online, offer coin purchasers the choice to obtain these sorts of coins at reduced prices. Auction sales typically take 3 to 4 months to process, depending upon how quick bidders are able to pick their bids.

Regardless of how popular auction sales have actually ended up being to lots of collectors, it is still essential to understand the benefits and disadvantages it can supply to coin collectors. Here are certain points which might have to be thought about prior to purchasing on auction sales.

Advantages

1. Auction sales have easier negotiations. An auction sale is the easiest way of purchasing coins. This is due to the set price that is scheduled for the coin. It is simpler to weigh alternatives and approximate the coin price.

2. Auction sales consist of a bidding procedure. Purchasers are just going to have to bid for the price they want to spend on a particular coin. This indicates that a coin is going to be obtained within the designated budget plan of the purchaser. If a purchaser truly likes a coin, then he could bid for a greater price to ensure that there is a greater probability of winning.

3. There is a greater likelihood of getting the product, particularly if the purchaser who won the bid was declined for some reason. This might additionally take place when the coin price was not

met. When this takes place, the item for bidding is generally passed in. This indicates that the product is not going to be offered, and the bidding is going to be re-opened any time soon.

4. Contracts are associated with the bidding procedure. When a purchaser won a bid on a particular coin, contracts are going to be exchanged right away between the the seller and bidder. This is going to ensure that the negotiation was finished and the bid price is going to be provided for the product.

5. The individual who has the highest bid is going to have the ability to make a deposit payment. This is going to make sure that the product is going to be booked for the individual who won the bid. Deposits might be a portion of the entire quantity of the coin.

Downsides

1. When purchasing on online auction sales, there is a greater tendency of scams. This is since the negotiation is performed on the web. The purchaser does not see the individual who is offering the

product or if the other bidders are actual individuals who are actually bidding for the product.

2. There are additionally times when the product that was shown on the site before the bid is not the identical product once it was shipped to the individual who won the bid. It is advised that the purchaser makes sure that the identical product that was bid for would be delivered to the consumer.

3. Online auctions will not guarantee the purchasers that what they are bidding for is a real item. The purchasers are just going to have the ability to examine the coin once they have actually won the bid, and the product was shipped to them. This generally causes fraud, and the purchasers wind up being sorry for why they even considered bidding for the product.

Auction sales might be popular, however, it is still highly encouraged that purchasers are knowledgeable about the advantages and disadvantages of this choice. It is additionally best that purchasers are familiar with their rights as customers and purchasers. Other choices might additionally be considered prior to picking the auction sale option.

Collectors might think about purchasing from buddies and agents whom they know. If they still wish to purchase on auction sales, they want to ensure that the site or the auction house has no records of unlawful activities. Purchasers might additionally spend a bit of time reading reviews about the sellers to ensure that they are doing business with reputable individuals.

Chapter 10: Commemorative and Other Special Coins

Commemorative coins have actually ended up being incredibly prominent these days. Many individuals wish to have various types of coins as their collections or keepsakes. They are even utilized as conventional presents to a special individual in any sort of event. Even though these coins are ruled out as practical presents, these commemorative products can be kept for many years as special keepsakes for a special buddy or a family member.

There is a strong need for these products amongst individuals who are collecting various sorts of coins. Most likely, these coins might have substantial meanings to them. Others get them due to the fact that they wish to remember a crucial day or event. The event and the date of the coin could be one aspect of why many individuals find them as collectible products.

In the 1970s, coins were readily available in the market each year. They exist in sets of special displays and bundles. Numerous collectors state that one reason might be the coin devaluation in 1971, or the strong emergence of the euro might have been among the variables why the coin was marketed.

There are nations which generate commemorative coins and utilize these coins to represent certain propaganda. There were families and monarchs in the greater societies who have actually unleashed previous or present occasions and events that might mark their authorities throughout those times.

The half-dollar was created in 1892 to provide significance to the Columbian Exposition in Chicago. This was an event where the US created a commemorative coin to mark this essential date which is now a portion of its history. It additionally honors the 400th anniversary of the Christopher Columbus' expedition and his discoveries on the planet.

The next year, the initial quarter dollar commemorative was presented to represent the Exposition, however, it additionally offered honor to

Spanish queen Isabella. She was the person who backpedaled the Women's Rights programs.

The initial commemorative coin which was created in silver was presented in the 1900s. The coin was created to honor Lafayette and George Washington. By the ensuing years, the half dollar coin was denominated, and the legal tender commemorative coins were chosen to mark events instead of historic occasions. These coins are acknowledged these days as special coins sets which have actually been historic between 1892 and 1954.

In 1932, the Washington quarter dollar was introduced as the United States' 2nd commemorative. It was released for the George Washington' 200th birth anniversary . The coin additionally carried on with its circulation as a commemorative coin since it stayed popular in the years after its denomination.

In 1975 the Bicentennial quarter was presented. It additionally ended up being the 2nd circulating commemorative coin in the nation, while the half dollars and silver dollars were reissued between

1776 and 1976. There was then the creation of the special edition.

These coins were crafted from base metal-copper nickel for the marketplace circulation.

Lots of collectors have various plans for collecting these coins. Some of them wish to opt for those 1892 to 1954 commemorative coins while a lot of collectors pick the contemporary editions. They do understand that these coins have various worths in their distinct editions and series.

Even though various series were launched, one more proposition was submitted to the congress to mark the Lincoln cent, most likely for his birth anniversary.

The complicated component of these commemoratives which are circulating is the denomination pattern. The 1776-1976 commemoratives silver dollar and half-dollar might not be included since the majority of those which are circulating are the quarter dollar ones. It ought to be an intriguing advancement for the proposed coin circulation.

Chapter 11: How and Where You Can Purchase Bullion Coins

Tips for Purchasing Bullion Coins

Bullion coins don't just have high value due to the fact that they are scarce. They might have additionally been discovered on shipwrecks, or they might originate from old times. The bullion coins are the kind of collector's products which many individuals try to find.

The silver bullion might be the most popular kind of bullion which is selling extremely well on the web, aside from those that are to be taken into consideration to be the most pricey and important products worldwide. Certain high priced coins which are shown on the web consist of the silver ingot. The silver ingot was stated to be discovered in the ship Spanish Atocha, which sank in the ocean. This ship had treasures and artifacts, which include the silver ingot coin. Lots of folks additionally declare that the silver ingots were recovered from the old Colorado Mining location. Coins were everywhere, and it was claimed that they were hidden by the residents throughout those durations.

The silver Maple Leaf Coins, that are sealed formally, are additionally prominent amongst collectors. These coins originated from the Royal Canadian Mint which consist of the Walking Liberty half-dollars and the dealer roll first-strike 1994 U.S. Eagles. These products were the Franklin'sMint collection.

The majority of bullion collectors choose the gold bullion. Some popular bullion gold coins consist of the gold Krugerrands, which were discovered in South Africa. The European gold crowns, nevertheless, were introduced in the late 1800s up to the early 1900s. Other products additionally consist of the United States American Eagle Coins and the Canadian Maple Leaf coins. British sovereigns are additionally primarily found on the web consisting of the French Roosters and Swiss Helveteas.

An incredible 10-ounce Swiss gold bar, American Eagle proof set, and China gold panda set coins could additionally be discovered and are additionally taken into consideration to be the most seen sites on the web. There are gold bullions discovered in the American Eagle set, Rounds, Mixed Lots, Bars, and any other comparable classifications that are discovered on some specific sites on the web.

A kind of bullion which is not that popular is the Platinum bullion. It is less investigated on the web due to the fact that it does not have the identical demand as the gold and silver bullions. Platinum bullions could be bought anywhere. A few of them are the Eagle sets, French Statue of Liberty coins, and the Koala Proofs. The World Trade Center has actually additionally provided certain Platinum bullions such as the crucible dish constructed from platinum bullion, Englehard Platinum bar, and the Johnson Matthew Year of the Dragon coin, that is recuperated from the structure's safety vaults after it collapsed.

They could be considered as thoughtful presents aside from them being pricey. They could be kept as a buddy's memento from the individual who granted it. A bullion bar with a happy birthday greeting could be a thoughtful present to a buddy's birthday, particularly if the bar has the date of the birthday on it.

Some individuals additionally utilize them for their anniversaries as their presents to one another. They look for those bullions which have the wedding year or the engagement date. Some brides additionally ask their groom to get her silver or gold flakes as her selected token for the wedding event.

This can truly cost an individual a great deal of cash in purchasing such costly bullions; however, here are some ideas that could assist an individual in his hunt for budget-friendly bullions.

1. An individual needs to know what kind of bullion he wants to acquire prior to buying from the shop.

2. He needs to ask the individual which bullion he likes and tell him/her to go with him to purchase the bullion.

3. An individual ought to have the ability to figure out the shipment expenses and the agreed price.

4. An individual ought to make certain that the seller would call them about the date the product is going to be shipped if they have actually purchased it on the web.

5. He must never make the payments in instantaneous cash transfer companies.

6. It is necessary to understand the seller's background in the bullion business.

An individual can acquire any bullion which he chooses. The idea of providing bullions to a special somebody could be really thoughtful, and it functions as memorabilia which are going to be kept through the years.

Chapter 12: Finding Fake Coins

How to Discover Fake Coins

A special device does the coin stamping to make them real. Individuals who counterfeit coins are well trained and have the capability to manipulate those uncommon coins, which have high worth amongst collectors. The most typical process in counterfeiting is putting fluid metal into molds which are going to leave die marks with breaking on the fake coin.

Those who are professionals in identifying fake coins have actually observed that the modifications seen in the coins have actually added, eliminated, and even changed the coin's date markings. If an individual believes that he remains in the ownership of a fake collectible coin, he can attempt to get his other collections, that are supposed to be authentic and have the identical worth. He could then contrast the two coins to see wheter there are any markings on the fake one.

If the coin's worth is more than 5 cents, search for corrugations in the external the coin edges. These are really thin railings on the the coins edges. They additionally call this "reeding." Authentic coins have extremely thin edges, and they are uniformly distinct if one is really watchful. Those coins which are fake could be differentiated if the edges are not sufficiently thin.

Should there be circumstances in which an individual has actually received a fake coin, he must not return the fake coin to the individual that sent it to him. He needs to attempt to delay the individual in any circumstance. If the individual runs, he needs to attempt to keep him in sight. He ought to remember the individual's clothing and physical look and attempt to remember if the individual has any buddy throughout the exchange. If they have a vehicle, get the vehicle's plate number and call the nearby authorities for assistance right away.

There are numerous things which could be taken into consideration when recognizing whether the coin is fake or not:

1. A coin restrike could be used to recognize verified coins. These coins are really dated earlier than those initially released by the nation that launched them with the identical or specific features such as those coins which are original.

2. Coins of a particular nation in ancient times are, in some cases, copied by another nation. An individual might believe that it is a forgery, however, it is not due to the fact that they would have been lawfully authorized in the nation where they came from.

3. Forgery could be related to a profit. It may be the primary goal of the counterfeiting syndicate. The federal government often utilizes forgery for a certain political propaganda, such as in the Second World War. The Germans created countless British and American banknotes for the intent of making money from them and destabilizing the opponent's financial circumstance.

4. Another recognized kind of fake coins are the replica coins. Replica merely suggests that the initial coins are copied with identical functions and

markings. Nevertheless, the typical fake coins have their distinctions that can be found by professionals. Some deliberately place the word "copy" on the sides of the coins. The majority of these replicas are utilized for academic functions and museum displays.

5. The Lebanese connection is stated to have a big creation of fake coins. These coins were discovered to be utilized to trick lots of museums, business leaders, collectors and other nations which are looking for their ancient lost coins.

6. The circulated intended forgery and the collector intended forgery are kinds of forgeries where the coin worth is token intended, and the face values are accepted, despite their illegality and intrusive, unimportant values.

It is essential to see a professional to identify if the coin is fake. A common individual could quickly find the incorrect metal utilized for counterfeiting. If the individual is a collector of such products, he ought to be more familiar with these coins. A collector has to be more worried about the uncommon collectible coins due to the fact that this is where counterfeiters gain. They go for the really valuable market where they could make money.

Chapter 13: How to Stay Clear of Scams

Tips on How to Stay Away From Scams

Lots of people delight in shopping on the web, where there are fantastic coins which could be discovered. An individual might do his shopping while he is at house due to the fact that it is so hassle-free and time-saving instead of heading out searching for shops which offer collectible coins and other keepsakes.

An individual can distinguish a live auction from those on the Web since live auctions entertain bidders which call for the greatest price when the time comes. Lots of people which are bidding on the web make their experience so enjoyable, and they are familiar with the techniques on how they would win a web auction.

There are online websites where an individual could purchase any product that might catch his/her interest. This is where many coin collectors buy their preferred coins. By browsing and discovering the product that they desire, they could, in fact, negotiate and make the payments via the Web.

Even though it could be too risky to rely on a seller who is unidentified to the purchaser, many individuals are still making deals and payments via this sort of online auction.

Fraud is usually frequent nowadays, though numerous internet sites that do business online claim that the danger of fraud is not a thing to stress over. They state that just 0.0025 percent of real instances of fraud occur online. That implies only that one out of 40,000 noted web deals might be a fraud. On the other hand, the FBI has its own investigations, which show that the figures are not correct. They claim that the danger of fraud is a lot of greater according to their stats.

An individual ought to trust the FBI for this protection. Even though one can state that most of the online coin selling is all truthful and reliable, the procedure in which the deal is made could be most likely doubtful and unpredictable. There are business deals, which are directly carrying out fraud. Aside from flea market dealers, in-person auctions, mail-order sellers and some coin shops, the Web has the best odds of pulling off a fraud.

One protection which a coin purchaser ought to be aware of is how to make a "feedback." By doing this, an individual could see the scores of other bidders, and he might compare his deal with the deals of the others. In case there is a great likelihood of a fraud with a negative feedback, the individual might withdraw his involvement in the auction.

An individual might additionally get ideas by trying to find those members who have actually left a "positive feedback" and compare it to the seller response. An individual can make an evaluation of what may be feasible helpful information from those responses. An individual should be cautious when it comes to any deal which is offered.

There are circumstances in which an individual is tricked into buying the product. The picture on the Internet showed the coin that an individual wishes to have; however, they delivered something else entirely. These cases resemble fraud. An individual needs to ensure that the product he saw on the picture is the same product that is going to be shipped to him. Here are some suggestions that are going to assist an individual in preventing fraud throughout a coin search on the web.

1. An individual ought to save the online image of the coin he wishes to buy. There are sellers who get rid of the title and the image of the product when a purchase has actually been made.

2. An individual ought to get the auction information and the description. It could either be e-mailed to the individual or sent out by means of postal mail.

3. If there are doubts concerning the auction, an individual ought to request an explanatory note. This is going to prevent misunderstanding and confusion on the part of the purchaser.

4. An individual can decline any deal where he believes the price offered on the coin is too much. One ought to know the market price of the particular coin and contrast it to the price which was offered throughout the online transaction.

These are just a few pointers which are going to guarantee an individual his safety when making any deals online. Fraud could occur to anybody, specifically those who have an interest in buying collectible coins online. It is essential to be informed and educated about the possibilities of coming across a fraud.

Chapter 14: How to Look After Your Coins

How to Look After Collectible Coins

There are collectors who particularly find traditional editions of the coin that have actually existed between 1892 and 1954. These coins have marked occasions or might represent the work of royalty throughout that era. There are those collectors that opt for the contemporary series which are really distinct also, nowadays. The 50-piece has been out since 1999. These are specifically produced editions available for collectors.

The majority of these coins are created from copper, and the majority of the time, a collector might experience issues in preserving their feature and look. An individual collecting these sorts of coins ought to find out how to preserve and take appropriate care of these pricey collections. Copper coins ought to be cleaned up properly and need to be protected the same way qualified collectors do that with their coins.

Professional collectors clean their coins by the procedure of positioning the coins in a container devoid of air density. This is a safe manner to protect the functions of the coins. Due to the coins' years of circulation, there are possibilities of building up coatings, crud, verdigris, and other issues that could be discovered on a coin's face. This might additionally induce the pitting and the existence of the rusty surface area of the copper on the coin. This is when the rusty parts ought to be eliminated effectively without scratching.

There are items that are offered particularly for coin cleaning. Coin providers have these sorts of items which are particularly created for coin upkeep and cleaning. The item is recognized to be MS70, that eliminates rusty parts and other surface dirt.

It is suggested to utilize rubber gloves for the hand safety. The MS70 could dry the skin; however, there is absolutely nothing to fret about since it is not that harmful to the skin. An individual can soak the coins in for a couple of days or weeks, depending upon the rust or whichever dirt exists on the surface.

A soft toothbrush might additionally assist in cleaning and eliminating any dirt which is on the coin surface. Anyone can see the enhancement in the look after it was soaked and cleaned up. If tidiness and look of the coin are not as they should be, baking soda could be used to neutralize the MS70.

After soaking, the coin may be dried utilizing a Blue Ribbon coin cleaner and preservative. It can be used with a coat and dried for a number of days. The damp parts can be cleaned using soft cotton balls.

If blemishing is found on the coin, Deller's Darkener could be utilized after soaking it with MS70. If the brand-new look of the coin is as it should be, then that coin can be added to the collection.

The following part would be keeping and protecting the collection. Here are certain suggestions on how to look after collections:

1. The coin ought to be shielded from direct exposure to any type of element. It is additionally

essential not to scratch the coins. They ought to be managed with care to prevent scratches on the coin surfaces.

2. It is fine to keep the coins on plastic pockets or cases which are created particularly for sets and collections. These pockets and cases could shield the coins from scratches and dirt.

3. Coins ought to be cleaned up effectively utilizing lemon juice, vinegar, ammonia, or alcohol.

4. If there is unwanted dirt which is tough to eliminate on the surface, chemical items for cleaning up like Tarnex might be utilized. This alternative might be utilized if lemon juice and vinegar were unable to get rid of the dirt.

5. It is really crucial to keep in mind that the worth of the coin might diminish if the coin has been cleaned up. It is advised to look for the guidance of a professional on other ways of maintaining a coin.

Lots of coin collectors think that an individual must never ever clean their collection due to the fact that the product is going to impact the surface area when administered to it. It is primarily advised that an individual understands how to maintain their collection and keep the coins dirt-free.

I hope that you enjoyed reading through this book and that you have found it useful. If you want to share your thoughts on this book, you can do so by leaving a review on the Amazon page. Have a great rest of the day.

Printed in Great Britain
by Amazon